Joseph Ato Forson

Tax Incidence and Poverty Reduction: Assessing the Effects of Taxes on Income Distribution in Thailand

Der GRIN Verlag publiziert seit 1998 wissenschaftliche Arbeiten von Studenten, Hochschullehrern und anderen Akademikern als eBook und gedrucktes Buch. Die Verlagswebsite www.grin.com ist die ideale Plattform zur Veröffentlichung von Hausarbeiten, Abschlussarbeiten, wissenschaftlichen Aufsätzen, Dissertationen und Fachbüchern.

Document Nr. V212606

Joseph Ato Forson

Tax Incidence and Poverty Reduction: Assessing the Effects of Taxes on Income Distribution in Thailand

GRIN Verlag

Die Deutsche Bibliothek verzeichnet diese Publikation in der Deutschen Nationalbibliografie; detaillierte bibliografische Daten sind im Internet über http://dnb.d-nb.de/ abrufbar.

1. Auflage 2013
Copyright © 2013 GRIN Verlag GmbH
http://www.grin.com
Druck und Bindung: Books on Demand GmbH, Norderstedt Germany
ISBN 978-3-656-41173-4

Tax Incidence and Poverty Reduction: Assessing the Effects of Taxes on Income Distribution in Thailand.

By:
Joseph Ato Forson
2013

DEDICATION

This research is dedicated to the Lord God Almighty for my life and the breath of life in me, and to my lovely wife and daughter Rosemary Afrakomah Forson and Benedicta Nhyira Forson whose invaluable support, encouragement and prayers have brought me this far.

Table of Contents

Abstract

This paper looks at the effects of taxes on income distribution in Thailand making use of the 2005 data from the Bureau of the Budget and other sources. We attempt to figure out if Thai tax system is pro poor or rich (i.e. progressive or regressive) among the various tax types on the five quintile income groups. This paper is used to ascertain which income group tend to pay more of their incomes as taxes. The paper also explores the relationship between tax incidence and poverty reduction on the one hand and indicators of access to education and health services and social outcomes on the other using simple measures of association. We conclude that based on the results of the tax system, the income distribution of Thai households became more equal on individual income tax, implying a gradual effort to bridge the income gap between the rich and the poor in Thailand. A pre-tax Gini coefficient of 0.3056 saw a marginal improvement, leading to a post-tax Gini coefficient of 0.2862 on post-tax (IIT), implying the situation on post-tax individual income shows an attempt by Thai government to have equality in individual incomes, and thereby bridging the income gaps. In general, the total post-tax coefficient ended at 0.3085 indicating, though efforts are being put in place by government to enhance the income situation of the poor, the effort according to our empirical results is marginal and have even worsened the income disparity situation by increasing income inequality to another level. The result confirms the distribution of income of Thai households became more unequal, and an indicative of a tax regime which is regressive at the end. We therefore make a number of policy recommendations on the ensuing situation.

Keywords: Tax System; Thailand; Progressivity; Regressive; Corporate Income tax; VAT; Individual income tax.

Acknowledgement

I am very grateful to Prof. Pornlapat Buracom, the lecturer for Fiscal and Monetary Policy Analysis and Management (DA 841), at the National Institute of Development Administration (NIDA). This research program would not have been possible without the well taught lectures and materials provided by Prof. Pornlapat Buracom, who doubles as the Director of International program at GSPA. The same appreciation goes to Prof. Suchitra, and Prof. Nuttakrit co-lecturers of Quantitative Analysis for the expert work done in exposing students to the intricacies of doing a good quantitative research with SPSS and Excel spreadsheet. This research program would not have also been possible without the contribution of my colleagues in class. To the Teaching Assistant, Mr. Rodwell Mzondi from Malawi, I say big thank you for the information and additional insight shed on the course. I also wish to acknowledge the endless efforts of the PhD administrative staffs of GSPA for their excellent administrative contributions to making this course a success.

1. General Overview

Every year, government prepares annual budget outlining governments' plan with respect to how much it intends spending, where and how the revenue is to be generated from. However, the increasing welfare needs couple with the rising demand of employment, infrastructure provision among others have intensified governments' responsibilities in the economy. Taxation is undoubtedly the most effective means of revenue generation. Tax revenue accounts for more than two-thirds of government annual revenue in most economies. To enhance balance of payment position of an economy, governments are encouraged to run a budget that is surplus rather than deficit, implying revenue should exceed expenditure. This is where taxation plays a critical role. Government has to devise several approaches in levying out the right tax to the right taxable group. Conversely, taxation or tax system in an economy at the same time has the clout to cause social instability, depending on the exact type of tax deployed by government. Some tax types will continue to worsen the plight of the poor and increase income inequality whereas others will otherwise try to bridge this gap, all depending on the right mixed of taxation used by government and what the intensions are.

Taxes can generally be classified into two: direct and indirect taxes. These classifications have been arrived at based on the ability of the tax payer to shift the tax burden to other people. If the burden of tax is more difficult to be shifted, it is called direct tax. On the other hand if the burden of tax can easily be shifted, it is called indirect tax. Two major steps are involved in the estimation of tax incidence. The first is to determine who is the bearer of the burden (burden shifting assumptions) and secondly, the allocation of the burden to households in different income classes.

Thailand, like most developing tend to collect only a few direct taxes to facilitate government's expenditure. Individual income tax and corporate income tax are the most common direct taxes deployed. Thai government tends to rely heavily on indirect tax such as VAT, import-export tax and excise tax which causes inequality in income distribution. Tax accounts for over 14% of the gross domestic product in Thailand[1]. Earlier research by Medhi Krongkaew (1979) and others on Thailand have shown this. In this assignment, we are capitalizing on the passage of time to re-determine the orientation of Thai tax system and its aftermath effect it has had on the income distribution between the poor and the rich and assess the nature and extent of income inequality.

2. Research Questions

Succinctly, this research seeks to find answers to the following questions;

- Which tax type is dominant in Thailand?
- Why is this type dominant?
- Is the incidence of taxation in Thailand pro-poor or pro-rich?
- What is the implication if the tax system is seen to be regressive or progressive?
- Who bears majority of the tax burden in Thailand?

2.1 Research Objectives

This research seeks to achieve these objectives;

I.   To determine who bears the burden of the tax in Thailand
II. To unravel exactly how much is borne by each income classe
III. To study the effects of taxes on income distribution in Thailand
IV. To make recommendations based on the results of the empirical findings to the Thai Government.

3. Methods for Calculating Tax Incidence

The method of tax incidence is calculated based on the consumption expenditure spent by each income class in a given year before and after the taxes are applied. The various types of taxes are captured and levied based on whether the tax is direct or indirect. In this study, we primarily made use of the 2005 tax data in Thailand from the Bureau of the Budget (Bangkok). We worked with these data as it relates to these tax types. The

---

[1] See Chalongphob et al (1988)

following are some of the tax types whose burden is shared in Thailand. Below are their definitions and explanations.

Individual Income Tax. Because individual income tax is a direct tax, the burden of this tax cannot be shifted to other people. Taxpayers are as are assumed to bear the entire burden. The burden of this tax is allocated in proportion to household expenditure on tax.

Corporate Income Tax. Whether the burden of this can be shifted depends on the competition in the market. Because in developing countries firms are operating in non-competitive market, the burden of this tax therefore can be passed on to the consumers. The burden of this tax is shifted to the consumer in proportion to household expenditure on general consumption of each income class.

General Sale Tax/ VAT. Because it is an indirect tax, the burden of this tax is shifted to consumers through the increasing in prices to the consumers. The burden of this tax is distributed in proportion to household expenditure on general consumption.

Excise Tax: this is an indirect tax; the burden is also shifted to the consumers. Tax on liquor and tobacco; the burden of these taxes are distributed as proportion to household expenditure on liquor and tobacco. Tax on gasoline, automobiles, and electronic appliances are distributed as proportion to household expenditure on transportation and communication.

Import-Export Taxes. Import tax is indirect tax. The burden is distributed in proportion to household expenditure on general consumption. Export tax is equal to zero in Thailand.

4. Empirical Results

The empirical estimates of the distributive impact of Thai public system in 2005 is presented in five different ways, namely (1) distribution of income by income classes, (2) Consumption expenditure spent by each income class (3) distributional effects of taxes by income class (4) the effective tax rates and (5) the change in household income distribution after tax and other public revenues.

4.1 Incomes Distribution by Income Classes
Household incomes can be categorized into five main income classes of a given population. In Thailand, the same has been done. Income is distributed among the lowest, low, middle, high and highest income groups with per monthly income. In this assignment, there is an estimated population of 15.8 million shared among the various quintile groups in equal proportion of 20% (i.e. 3,160,000). Table 1 below shows this distribution.

Table 1: Distribution of income by income class

Income class	% of household	Income per month (Baht)	% of income
	Total = 15.8 million		
1. Lowest income	20% (3,160, 000)	4,197	8.16
2. Low income	20%(3,160,000)	6,259	12.17
3. Middle income	20%(3, 160,000)	8,364	16.26
4. High income	20%(3, 160,000)	11,279	21.93
5. Highest income	20%(3, 160,000)	21,335	41.48
Total	100.0%	51,434	100.0

Source: Author's own construct based on 2005 data, (2013)

Table 1 above shows the quintile income distribution by households in Thailand. 8.16% of income (approximately 4,197 baht per month per household) is earned by the lowest 20% of the total household (15.8 million) whereas 41.48% of income distribution is earned by the top 20% of household income group with an approximate monthly income of 21,335 baht per month. This table suggests income distribution in Thailand is pro-rich with the rich controlling more than 79% (see variable 3, 4, and 5) of the total household income of 51, 434 baht per month of total monthly income.

4.2 Expenditure by each income class in proportion

Individual incomes as represented among the various quintile groups are expended on four different functional areas. Out of these functional areas, government is able to levy taxes either directly or indirectly.

Table 2: Consumption expenditure spent by each income class   (in %)

Income class	Proportion of income spent on individual income tax	Proportion of income spent on general consumption	Proportion of income spent on liquor and tobacco	Proportion of income spent on transportation & communication
1. Lowest income	1.87	10.17	9.1	8.7
2. Low income	2.08	13.18	11.2	10.1
3. Middle income	16.32	18.74	15.6	14.7
4. High income	20.56	20.25	26.9	20.0
5. Highest income	59.17	37.66	37.2	46.5
Total	100.0	100.0	100.0	100.0

Source: Author's own construct based on 2005 data, (2013)

The consumption expenditure pattern in table 2 shows that, like most developing countries, consumption expenditure is spent by individual income class on individual income tax, general consumption, liquor and tobacco and transportation and communication. The table mirrors the income distribution pattern in table 1 affirming the point, the higher income one earn reflects in the expenditure pattern of that income class. The lowest income class expend 10.17% of their income on general consumption whiles expending 1.87% of their income on individual income tax. The middle income class spends almost 18.74% of their total income on individual income tax as against 14.7% expended on transportation and communication. The high income earners expended over 26.9% of the total income earnings on liquor and tobacco and 20% on transportation and communication. The highest income class paid more of their income earnings as individual tax (approximately 59.17%) and expended less on liquor and tobacco (approximately 37.2%).

In general, the highest income class tends to expend more of their incomes on the enlisted functional consumption areas. On individual income tax, it's obvious from this table that the tax system in Thailand is pro-rich. The income group that earns high income tends to pay more on income tax (direct tax) implying the tax incidence on individual income tax is progressive. The other functional areas replicated the same scenario for all income class.

4.3 Distributional Effects of Taxes by income classes

Below is the distribution of taxes on the income classes.

Table 3: Calculating the distributional effects of taxes by income class (million baht)

Type of tax	Total Amount (2005)	Income class				
		Lowest income	*Low income*	*Middle income*	*High income*	*Highest income*
1. Individual income tax	153, 920	2,878.30	3,201.54	25,119.74	31,645.95	91,074.46
2. Corporate income tax	288,500	29,340.45	38,024.30	54,064.90	58,421.25	108,649.10
3. VAT	376,400	38,279.88	49,609.52	70,537.36	76,221.00	141,752.24
4. Excise tax	-	-	-	-	-	-
5. Import tax	-	-	-	-	-	-
Total	818,820	70,498.63	90,835.36	149,722.00	166,288.20	341,475.80
Percent	100.0	8.61	11.09	18.29	20.31	41.70

Source: Author's own construct based on 2005 data, (2013)

Table 3 shows the distributional effects of taxes by income class in billion baht. Thai government accrues over 818,820 million baht revenue from taxes among the taxable income groups. This total amount is generated from the various tax types in Thailand (i.e. individual income tax, corporate income tax etc., see column 1 above). Value Added Tax (VAT), which is an indirect tax commands over 376, 400 million baht of the total amount accrued on tax revenue. The highest income group bore a hefty proportion of the VAT type of tax with an estimated amount of 141,752.24 million baht of their incomes paid as VAT to government. 41.70% (or 341, 475.80) of the total government revenue in effect was generated from the highest income group. The lowest income household paid only 8.61% (70,498.63 million baht) as tax revenue to government whereas 18.29% (149,722.00 million baht) was generated from middle income earners as tax revenue.

In general sense, given the number of households in each income group to be the same, it makes it easier to compare the burden of each tax by income classes. The table suggests that the tax system in Thailand is still progressive in nature as the rich continues to pay more than the poor in absolute terms. In addition, indirect tax still dominants tax type seen through the hefty contribution to revenue from VAT and corporate tax. However, looking at the absolute figures alone is not enough to conclude whether the tax system is progressive or regressive. A lot more of the analysis needs to be done to paint a clearer picture.

Alternatively, another way of calculating the distributive impact of a public revenue system is to divide the absolute tax burden of each income class by the total income of that class. The result is called the effective tax rate.

4.4 Effective Tax Rate

Effective tax rate is the ratio of absolute burden of tax to the total (money) income of the households which bear such burden. In other words, it shows the proportion of money income that each income class has contributed, directly or indirectly, as taxes, charges or other payments to the government. Table 4 presents such effective tax rates by income class, by each major type of tax.

Table 4: Calculating the Effective tax rate (%)

Type of tax	Income class				
	Lowest income	*Low income*	*Middle income*	*High income*	*Highest income*
1. Individual income tax	1.81	1.35	7.92	7.4	11.26
	18.44	16.02	17.05	13.66	13.43
2. Corporate income tax	24.05	20.9	22.24	17.82	17.52
3. VAT	-	-	-	-	-
4. Excise tax	-	-	-	-	-
5. Import tax					
Percent	*44.30*	*38.27*	*47.21*	*38.88*	*42.21*

Source: Author's own construct based on 2005 data, (2013)

The average effective tax rate for the whole revenue system is estimated to be 42.17%, indicating the fiscal burden of Thai government upon households was almost 42% of their total money income.

The effective rates seen above can also be used as an indicator of the progressivity of the tax and other revenue systems. If the effect tax rate increases as family income increases, it means that the revenue system in question is progressive. On the other hand, if the tax rate decreases while family income increases, the system is regressive. Regressive revenue system would, in general, worsen the existing income distribution, whereas progressive system would improve it. From table 4, it is obvious that the system of tax is regressive as the highest effective rate was recorded in the middle income earners (47.21%) whiles the least recorded was 38.27% for the low income group. Though there is an indication of the individual income effective tax rate increasing, suggesting progressivity, the other two tax types had effective rates that were decreasing, also suggesting regressive nature of the tax system (see figure 1). In general, there is an attempt to shift the tax burden to the poor by all indication as the lowest and middle income groups recorded a total of 44.30%, 38.27% and 47.21% effective rates respectively as opposed to the high and highest income classes.

Figure 1: Effective tax rate

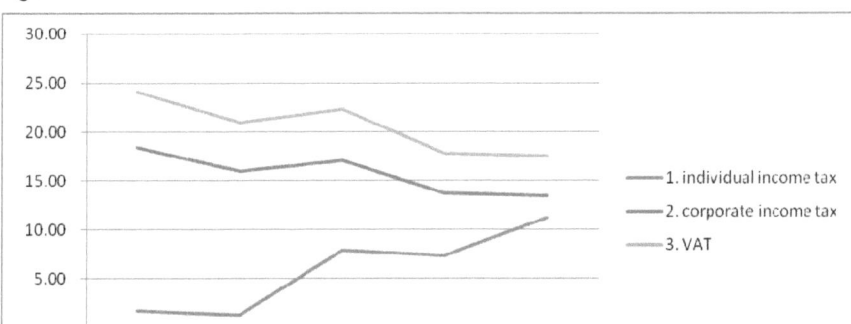

Source: Author's own construct, 2013.

Figure 1 represents all the three tax types administered in Thailand in revenue mobilization. Individual income tax shows a trend which is increasing in nature to suggest progressive revenue system. The other two tax types suggest a decreasing trend (corporate income tax and VAT) as the burden is shifted to the poor (regressive).

4.5 Post-Tax Income Distribution

An important aspect of a tax and other revenue incidence study is to ascertain how such a public revenue system has changed the existing income distribution. By deducting the absolute tax burden from appropriate household income, one obtains the "post-tax" income. Relative positions of these post-tax incomes across all income classes give a new picture of the distribution of income of the same households. When the new distribution shows an improvement in income equality, then the tax policies that caused such change were desirable. The table below shows the pre and post tax effects of the various tax types on the income classes.

Table 5: Calculating post-tax income distribution before and after tax (% of total income)

Income Class	Pre-Tax	Post-Tax (IIT)	Post-Tax(CIT)	Post-Tax (VAT)	Post-Tax (Total) absolute	Post-Tax(Total)
1. Lowest income	8.16	8.7	7.81	7.68	88,651,610,000	7.83
	12.17	13.03	11.99	11.93	146,505,920,000	12.95
2. Low income	16.26	16.26	15.83	15.67	167,440,880,000	14.80
	21.93	22.05	22.22	22.33	261,411,480,000	23.10
3. Middle income	41.48	39.96	42.14	42.39	467,547,400,000	41.32
4. High income						
5. Highest income						
Total	100.00	100.00	100.00	100.00	1,131,557,290,000	100.00
Gini coefficient	0.3056	0.2862	0.3156	0.3193		0.3085

Source: Author's own construct based on 2005 data, (2013)

The table above shows the effect of Thai tax system on the various income classes. The income share of the lowest income group increased from 8.16% to 8.7% on individual income tax and decreased from 7.81% to 7.68% on corporate and VAT taxes with a post-tax total absolute of 88,651,610,000 baht, indicating the income position of the poor improved initially, but worsened on corporate and VAT. On the other hand, the middle income group saw a stable situation in income from initial pre-tax of 16.26% to post-tax 16.26% (IIT) and subsequently worsened on the other tax types with an approximate post-tax absolute of 167,440,880,000 baht. The highest income group had a pre-tax of 41.48% to 39.96% (IIT) and increased to 42.14% (CIT) and 42.39% (VAT), but a post-tax total of 41.32% indicating a marginal worsening situation in the position of this income group. Though, tax burden on individual income tax indicate tax unequal, but CIT and VAT saw a general improvement. The tax system of Thailand has succeeded in redistributing the income from rich families to poor families, since there is an attempt to have the rich pay more hence bridging the income gap- a kind of "pro-poor" rather than "pro-rich" tax and revenue system on IIT tax type most especially.

To have a better picture of this, we estimated the pre-tax and post-tax Gini coefficients in table 5 from data in table 4. We conclude that based on the results of the tax system, the income distribution of Thai households became more equal on individual income tax, implying a gradual effort to bridge the income gap between the rich and the poor in Thailand. A pre-tax Gini coefficient of 0.3056 saw a marginal improvement, leading to a post-tax Gini coefficient of 0.2862 on post tax (IIT), implying the situation on post tax individual income shows an attempt by Thai government to have equality in individual income, and thereby bridging the income gaps. In general, the total post tax coefficient ended at 0.3085 indicating, though efforts are being put in place by government to enhance the income situation of the poor, the effort according to our empirical results is marginal and have even worsened the income disparity situation by increasing income inequality to another level. The result confirms the distribution of income of Thai households became more unequal. Though the ensuing empirical results are an improvement over Medhi Krongkaew (1979) findings, it appears the general conclusion here is akin to Medhi's findings as the tax system across the tax types shows a mixed finding, but indicative of a tax system which is generally regressive at the end.

5. Policy Recommendations

The tax system in Thailand is somewhat regressive allowing the poor to pay more as taxes as oppose to the rich. Tax reform is the basic recommendation that most economist would suggest for effective policy changes. In most developing countries like Thailand, making such a recommendation will warrant a careful study of the entire tax system for distributive purposes and that is exactly what we have succeeded in doing in this paper. On the basis of this, the following recommendations are being outlined as a measure to address the glaring income disparities in Thailand.

Effort should be made to widen the type of taxes available. As long as Thai government still has to depend on indirect taxes as its major sources of revenue, the chance of improving existing income distribution by tax policies is rather slim. Thai government must attempt to put less emphasis on indirect taxes as sources of revenue. However, the use of indirect tax as a major way to discourage certain consumption can still be practiced as long as certain consumptions are highly income elastic but not as pretext to extract more revenue.

Another way of reducing emphasis on indirect taxes is to change the way the tax is collected. More emphasis ought to be given to individual income tax. To achieve this, efforts should be made to undertake reform to improve tax administration, increased checks on tax evasion, wider definition of income, less preferential treatments of certain incomes such as income from professional activities. Currently, the present tax rates on the income classes look reasonable.

In addition, efforts should be made to bridge the income gap by taxing the rich and wealthy class. Though in this study, we saw glimpses of that, we still are of the opinion there is more to be done. There should be an attempt to levy taxes on wealth and property in Thailand. This is the only way to reduce income inequality. Capital gain from the stock market investors should be captured in the tax bracket.

Since VAT (a variant of indirect tax) was seen to command high tax revenue to Thai government, usually levied on public activities like lotteries, distilleries and tobacco are seen to be too burdensome to lower-income households. In place of trying to generate more revenue from these income classes, other measures like government nationwide sensitization programs could be organized to dissuade people from the consumption of these products.

REFERENCE

Apps Patricia (1981), "A *theory of inequality and taxation*", Cambridge [England]: Cambridge University Press, 1981. 0521234379

Chalongpholo Sussangkarn, Pranee Tinakorn and Tienchai Chongpeerapien (1988), "*The tax structure in Thailand and its distributional implications*", TDRI

Hamid R. Davoodi, Ervin R. Tiongson and Sawitree Sachjapinan Asawanuchit (2010), "*Benefit Incidence of Public Education and Health Spending Worldwide: Evidence from a New Database*" Poverty & Public Policy, Vol.2 Issue 2

Khalizadeh- Shirazi, Javad Shah Anwar (1991), "*Tax Policy in Developing Countries*", Washington, D.C.: World Bank, c1991

Medhi Krongkaew (1979), *the distributive impact of Government's policies: An Assessment of the situations in Thailand*, Faculty of Economics, Thammasat University Bangkok 2, Thailand.

OECD Committee on fiscal Affairs (1981), "*The impact of consumption taxes at different income levels: a report*". Paris: Organisation for Economic Co-operation and Development; [Washington, D.C.: available from OECD Publications and Information Center, c1981] 9264122125 (pbk.).

Pornlapat Buracom (2011), "*the determinants and distributional effects of public education, health and welfare spending in Thailand*", Asian Affairs: an American review vol.38, no.3, 113

APPENDIX

Effective Tax Rate

$$ETR = \frac{\text{Total amount of each tax paid by each income class} * 100}{(\text{Total income per year of each income class}) * (\text{Total amount of household in each income class})}$$

Post- Tax income Distribution
Household's income of each income
class after tax = [Total income of each income class] - [Taxes paid by each income class]

Total income of each income
class = [Total income per year of each income class] * [Total amount of household in each income class]

$$GINI\ COEFFICIENT = 1 + \frac{1}{N} - 2[\frac{Nx1 + (N-1)X2 + \cdots .. + 2XN - 1 + xn}{NX}]$$

Where;
N = amount of income class
X = proportion of income of total income class
X = proportion of income in each income class
I = 1,2,....n (income class)